Cybercrime

Other titles in the Crime Scene Investigations series:

Cybercrime

by Kevin Hile

LUCENT BOOKS

A part of Gale, Cengage Learning

GALE
CENGAGE Learning

Detroit • New York • San Francisco • New Haven, Conn • Waterville, Maine • London

LIBRARY OF CONGRESS CATALOGING-IN-PUBLICATION DATA

Hile, Kevin.
  Cybercrime / by Kevin Hile.
    p. cm.—(Crime scene investigations)
  Includes bibliographical references and index.
  ISBN 978-1-4205-0107-0 (hardcover)
  1. Computer crimes—Juvenile literature. I. Title.
  HV6773.H55 2009
  364.16'8--dc22

                                                 2009019101

Lucent Books
27500 Drake Rd
Farmington Hills MI 48331

ISBN-13: 978-1-4205-0107-0
ISBN-10: 1-4205-0107-0

Printed in the United States of America
1 2 3 4 5 6 7 13 12 11 10 09

Printed by Bang Printing, Brainerd, MN, 1ˢᵗ Ptg., 12/2009

Contents

Foreword

The popularity of crime scene and investigative crime shows on television has come as a surprise to many who work in the field. The main surprise is the concept that crime-scene analysts are the true crime solvers, when in truth, it takes dozens of people, doing many different jobs, to solve a crime. Often, the crime-scene analyst's contribution is a small one. One Minnesota forensic scientist says that the public "has gotten the wrong idea. Because I work in a lab similar to the ones on *CSI*, people seem to think I'm solving crimes left and right—just me and my microscope. They don't believe me when I tell them that it's just the investigators that are solving crimes, not me."

Crime-scene analysts do have an important role to play, however. Science has rapidly added a whole new dimension to gathering and assessing evidence. Modern crime labs can match a hair of a murder suspect to one found on a murder victim, for example, or recover a latent fingerprint from a threatening letter, or use a powerful microscope to match tool marks made during the wiring of an explosive device to a tool in a suspect's possession.

Probably the most exciting of the forensic scientist's tools is DNA analysis. DNA can be found in just one drop of blood, a dribble of saliva on a toothbrush, or even the residue from a fingerprint. Some DNA analysis techniques enable scientists to tell with certainty, for example, whether a drop of blood on a suspect's shirt is that of a murder victim.

While these exciting techniques are now an essential part of many investigations, they cannot solve crimes alone. "DNA doesn't come with a name and address on it," says the Minnesota forensic scientist. "It's great if you have someone in custody to match the sample to, but otherwise, it doesn't help.

That's the investigator's job. We can have all the great DNA evidence in the world, and without a suspect, it will just sit on a shelf. We've all seen cases with very little forensic evidence get solved by the resourcefulness of a detective."

While forensic specialists get the most media attention today, the work of detectives still forms the core of most criminal investigations. Their job, in many ways, has changed little over the years. Most cases are still solved through the persistence and determination of a criminal detective whose work may be anything but glamorous. Many cases require routine, even mind-numbing tasks. After the July 2005 bombings in London, for example, police officers sat in front of video players watching thousands of hours of closed-circuit television tape from security cameras throughout the city, and as a result were able to get the first images of the bombers.

The Lucent Books Crime Scene Investigations series explores the variety of ways crimes are solved. Titles cover particular crimes such as murder, specific cases such as the killing of three civil rights workers in Mississippi, or the role specialists, such as medical examiners, play in solving crimes. Each title in the series demonstrates the ways a crime may be solved, from the various applications of forensic science and technology to the reasoning of investigators. Sidebars examine both the limits and possibilities of the new technologies and present crime statistics, career information, and step-by-step explanations of scientific and legal processes.

The Crime Scene Investigations series strives to be both informative and realistic about how members of law enforcement—criminal investigators, forensic scientists, and others—solve crimes, for it is essential that student researchers understand that crime solving is rarely quick or easy. Many factors—from a detective's dogged pursuit of one tenuous lead to a suspect's careless mistakes to sheer luck to complex calculations computed in the lab—are all part of crime solving today.

New Technology, New Crimes

When computers and the Internet first came into common use in the 1980s and 1990s, they were hailed as bringing in a new era of efficient, paperless offices and democratic free speech through the World Wide Web. That freedom of communication and secure electronic storage of data that once promised so much has, since then, come under attack by criminals who have learned to use the technology for everything from personal gain to computer data vandalism.

Today a great deal of time, effort, and money is being spent by computer users of all types in order to protect themselves from these criminals. Most people who use computers are now aware that they need to install security software, such as antivirus protection and firewalls. These programs need constant updating and monitoring and have to be run regularly to check that computers are safe to use. Many people also are aware of the hazards of e-mail messages that may look innocent but are malicious software that may wipe out the memory on a hard drive or steal personal information.

The Era of Cybercrime

Today news reports warning computer users to be wary of a new threat are common. On July 30, 2008, for example, the Federal Bureau of Investigation (FBI) issued an alert for people to watch out for the Storm Worm spam e-mail. The message appears to offer information about the Facebook online social network and the FBI, but when users click a link in the text, a Web site opens that downloads a computer worm onto their hard drive. Like victims in a bad 1960s zombie movie, these computers have now been taken over by a master computer that controls their operations.

A police officer works on a computer during a program on computer forensic education. Computer-assisted crimes are often investigated by computer forensics teams.

While computer viruses and e-mail spam are what usually spring to mind when people think about computer crime, almost any type of crime can be aided with the use of technology. This includes everything from identity theft to sexual harassment to hate crimes. Police and federal law enforcement agencies have been struggling to keep up with this growing trend. They use

9

the new field of computer forensics to battle these cyber bad guys. Sometimes, though, it is hard for the average person to be sure who the bad guys are and who the good guys are, because cybercrooks have mastered the ability to disguise themselves as other people, companies, and even law enforcement.

Computer forensics can go a long way in unraveling the complex digital clues that cybercriminals leave behind. The discipline combines fields that have become very exciting for young people considering a career in law enforcement: computer science and traditional crime-scene investigation methods. This specialty of forensics, however, is not for everyone. It takes a lot of training, discipline, and technical know-how. Yet for those who are up to the challenge, it can be a rewarding and profitable career choice; one that is likely to be in high demand as long as criminals and high-tech gadgetry exists.

CHAPTER 1

What Is Cybercrime?

Crime has been a social problem since the beginning of human history. Computer technology, however, is a modern development that has only recently become a useful tool for clever criminals. Because "cybercrime" is on the cutting edge of law enforcement, police, federal agents, and the legal system are constantly being challenged by unexpected uses of this technology. People who fight cybercrime often rely on computer forensics to track down perpetrators.

The word *cybercrime* is a catchall term for many types of criminal behavior involving computers and other types of high-tech equipment. The prefix "cyber-" stems from the word *cyberspace*, which was coined by author William Gibson in his 1984 science-fiction novel, *Neuromancer*. Gibson wrote of a virtual world that existed within computers and computer networks. Cybercrime, then, refers to crimes that are perpetrated using computer technology and exist primarily in cyberspace. Sometimes such crimes are performed on-site, such as on a computer located at a business. These days, however, lawbreakers commonly use the Internet for their illegal activities.

A Veil of Anonymity

One unique characteristic of cybercrime is its anonymity. Before advanced computer networks and the Internet came into existence, a person had to perpetrate an illegal activity in person. A notable exception is mail fraud, or using letters or other published material sent through the postal service to commit crimes that, typically, involve money deals. Cybercriminals, when caught, often are prosecuted using mail fraud laws. Today,

Cyberbullies and Vigilantes

Cyberbullies harass people online. In Pennsylvania in 2006, before the state had a law against cyberbullying, a group of teenagers set up a MySpace Web page about a sixteen-year-old girl that included a lot of malicious gossip and photographs that had been digitally altered. In another case, this time in New Zealand, a teenager was harassed by hateful text messages to the point where he could not take it anymore and he committed suicide.

Cybervigilantes are people who use the Internet to wage a campaign of justice against people they think are criminals. Cybervigilantes will make these people's names public—on blogs, in chat rooms, and in message boards—without due process of law.

On a National Public Radio broadcast, Daniel Solove, author of the book, *The Future of Reputation: Gossip, Rumor, and Privacy on the Internet*, noted that there are entire Web sites devoted to Internet shaming, where bloggers post remarks on everything from people who do not leave good tips at restaurants to people who cheat on their spouses, boyfriends, or girlfriends.

however, lawbreakers can steal, scam, destroy information, and hurt people in other ways without the victims ever seeing the perpetrator or even knowing his or her name.

The dangerous result is that potential criminals feel less inhibited because they can hide behind a mask of anonymity. With their identities hidden, people who might not otherwise commit a crime are more likely to do so. Cyberspace anonymity also makes tracking criminals a bigger challenge for detectives, since inventive lawbreakers are finding new ways all the time to prevent policing agencies from locating them.

Another problem with cybercrime is that the activities committed can be so new that the legal system has not created laws against them yet. Thus, the activities cannot be prosecuted as crimes. For example, cyberbullying (harassing people—usually teens or young adults—over the Internet, by e-mail, in chat rooms, or on Web sites) was a crime in only nine states (Arkansas, Idaho, Iowa, Missouri, New Jersey, New York, Oregon, Rhode Island, and Vermont) as of 2008.

Many Types of Cybercrime

David S. Wall, professor of criminal justice at the University of Leeds in England, categorizes computer crimes into three types: computer-integrity crimes, computer-assisted crimes, and computer-content crimes. In his book, *Cybercrime: The Transformation of Crime in the Information Age,* Wall writes that computer-integrity crimes "include hacking and cracking, vandalism, spying, denial of service, the planting and use of viruses and trojans." Wall also writes, "Computer-assisted crimes use networked computers to commit crimes, usually to acquire money, goods or services dishonestly," and that computer-content "crimes are related to the illegal content on networked computer systems and include the trade and distribution of pornographic materials as well as the dissemination of hate crime materials."[1]

Within these categories, cybercrimes can take many forms. One of the most common types of illegal activity is a computer virus. Viruses are mini-programs that invade a computer's hard drive. The purpose is either to deliberately damage the computer and make it impossible to use or to steal information that is on the computer. Related to viruses are trojans, programs that create backdoors (viruses and trojans that create an opening to a computer that allows other malware to enter) that allow criminals to more easily attack a computer, and worms, programs that reproduce themselves within a

By the Numbers

206,884

Number of complaints about computer crimes filed at the Internet Crime Complaint Center in Washington, D.C., in 2007

computer and spread through a computer network or through the Internet. Together, viruses, trojans, and worms are called malicious software, or malware for short.

When someone mentions illegal computer activity, malicious software is what usually comes to mind. But there are many other ways that criminals can use technology to commit illegal—or just plain annoying—activities. Among these are sending spam e-mails or posting messages in chat rooms or on message boards, luring people into business scams or other illegal activities. This method of enticing computer users into a trap is called social engineering. By pretending to be a potential friend or business partner, cybercrooks can lead the unwary into illegal business scams or to pornographic or other illicit Web sites.

In addition to damaging property and stealing information, cybercriminals can alter data to their own advantage. This is called data diddling, and it is an old practice. In one case from the late 1960s, corporate leaders at the investment company Equity Funding Corporation of America devised a plan to offer investors the opportunity to buy insurance policies and mutual funds at the same time. At first, they were highly successful, but when profits did not match the forecasts they were providing to investors, the company changed the data in their computer database. They created fictional sales of insurance policies at an unbelievably high rate. In the article, "The Equity Funding Fraud" for *Network World Security Newsletter*, M. E. Kabay, associate professor at Norwich University in Vermont, writes, "By late 1972, the head of data processing calculated that by the end of the decade, at this rate, Equity Funding would have insured the entire population of the world. Its assets would surpass the gross national product of the planet. The president [of the company] merely insisted that this showed how well the company was doing."[2] In 1972 a disgruntled Equity Funding employee reported the fraud to the U.S. Securities and Exchange Commission, a government agency established to protect investors from unfair trade and market practices, and the company's officers were arrested.

In the Equity Funding case, the illegal actions were sanctioned by the company's officers. Company employees can act independently too, changing or destroying corporate data in, for example, acts of revenge against their employers. A typical example is when an employee is fired from his or her job and attempts to steal or destroy company property. To prevent this, companies will often deny an employee access to computers just before firing him or her.

Zombies, Botnets, and DDoS

Once a backdoor is accomplished, the victim computer can be converted into a zombie computer. *Zombie* is the name given to a computer that has been taken over by a malicious program in order to spread more viruses and worms throughout a network. A network of infected zombie computers is often referred to as a botnet.

Trojans and botnets can combine to create a form of cyberattack known as a distributed denial of service attack (DDoS). When a DDoS attack is sent out over the Internet, it targets computer servers, making requests for Web site pages to be accessed, for example. It makes so many requests so rapidly, that the server cannot handle the load and crashes. One famous DDoS attack, known as MyDoom, appeared to target the UNIX operating system SCO.com in 2004 (law enforcement agencies could only speculate why this was the case). However, it also invaded thousands of computers outside the SCO company.

MyDoom sent out e-mails with subject lines that looked like an error message was being sent to the recipient. An attachment that appeared to be a text message was actually a disguised executable file. Once opened and downloaded, the MyDoom virus did a couple of things: It replicated itself and continued to send out numerous e-mails in a DDoS attack that jammed up servers and caused them to crash, and it placed a program on the user's computer that recorded keystrokes, allowing the creator of the virus to record private credit card and other useful information. The creator of the MyDoom virus was never caught.

Viruses, Worms, and Trojans

When not accessing computers directly, cybercriminals do so remotely using programs such as viruses. Early viruses were passed from computer to computer via floppy disks. Unsuspecting users would receive a computer disk from a friend or colleague, insert it into a drive, and the virus would download as soon as the disk was accessed. Viruses are usually executable files (they can often be recognized by their ".exe" file extensions) and so must be accessed or run, often by opening a file or clicking a hyperlink, in order to work. Today these viruses are spread primarily through e-mail and Web sites.

Many viruses damage data on a computer. However, some of the first viruses were written by programmers and academics who did not intend to cause any mischief. The Brain virus was written by software vendors Basit and Amjaad Farooq Alvi, who created a program that left their calling card (a file containing text deliberately identifying the person who gained access) on people's computers. They wrote the virus to see where their business address ended up, and thus pinpoint computers that were potentially downloading their proprietary software illegally.

Computer worms are similar to viruses, except that they can spread by themselves, because they spread through network connections, rather than through e-mails or file sharing. The Internet Worm virus, which was one of the first worms, was written in 1988 by Robert Morris, a student at Cornell University. Morris created the program to study how such programs spread, but unfortunately, he wrote some incorrect code. The virus ended up spreading throughout the Internet, effectively rendering computers inoperable.

Other famous viruses include the Michelangelo virus, which caused about ten thousand computers to crash on March 6 (the artist's birthday) in 1992. The Love Bug virus was distributed by e-mail in 2000 through Microsoft's Outlook program. The subject line displayed the tempting message, "I Love You," prompting the unsuspecting recipient to open the e-mail. Once opened, the virus downloaded onto the computer; destroyed data, especially media files; stole e-mails; and replicated itself in order to spread to other computers. Philippino computer student Onel de Guzman was blamed for causing billions of dollars in damage worldwide. De Guzman was a student at the AMA Computer College in Manila. He wrote a thesis paper about creating a virus that would allow people to get into pay sites without paying. He maintained, though, that the Love Bug virus was accidentally released and that he did not author it. However, it was suspected that the

Opening an e-mail with the Love Bug virus in 2000 caused widespread damage to computer files, at the expense of billions of dollars.

virus, which resembled the one described in his thesis, was let loose by de Guzman out of revenge when the college rejected his thesis. The Philippine government later dropped charges against him due to insufficient evidence.

Trojans are named after the Trojan horse of mythology. In the ancient Greek myth, the Achaeans tricked the citizens of Troy into letting them inside the city walls by presenting the gift of a large wooden horse. When the Trojans pulled the horse inside their gates, enemy soldiers hidden inside the horse broke out and attacked.

Trojan programs work in a similar fashion. They appear to be legitimate programs or files provided by someone known to the computer user. Trojans, unlike viruses, do not replicate themselves. Once opened, however, they can cause serious damage to a computer, or, more often, they insert a backdoor program that allows a criminal to then more easily access the computer's files.

Viruses and other malware also can be distributed by spam, or unsolicited e-mail. Spam also can be used to prompt e-mail recipients to click on a hyperlink to a Web site that prompts the visitor to input personal information about himself or herself. Such Web sites can be cleverly designed to appear like legitimate sites, such as those run by banks, financial advisers, or credit card companies.

Malware also can infect Web servers via chat rooms, message boards, and discussion groups. The 1999 Melissa virus, for example, was first spread by people who visited a Use.net discussion group, where people thought they were getting free access to pornography sites by downloading a list of passwords. Once these initial users downloaded the virus, it quickly spread through e-mails.

White Hats and Black Hats

Cybercrime—or, at least, a somewhat primitive form of it—began even before there were large networks and the Internet. Criminals could, for example, access information on a stand-alone computer and steal important data. This was the type of crime that began to trouble businesses during the early days of the technology revolution.

When computers first began to be used, the majority of those breaking into computer databases and networks did so because they wished to prove their programming skills. In essence, they wanted to show off what they could do to their fellow programmers. Sometimes, too, hacking into computers was done in order to test network and database security. Corporations, lawyers, and others hired skilled hackers, called "samurai," to conduct legal computer surveillance, serve as advisers in court cases, or help businesses or law agencies access systems for legal investigative purposes.

Did the internet just cause Sarah Palin to destroy evidence? The potential Veep is in a bit of trouble for conducting state business using her personal, unarchived email address (gov.sarah@yahoo.com) instead of her official

Such hackers—sometimes called "white hats" because they are seen as the good guys—still exist today. Sometimes they are appreciated by law enforcement, but some hackers who see themselves as the good guys are still regarded as criminals. For example, in September 2008, it was reported that hackers had broken into Republican vice presidential candidate Sarah Palin's Yahoo account and posted the results of her searches on the Internet. These so-called hactivists—a type of white hat who access Web sites illegally for a political cause—broke into Palin's account in an attempt to prove that she was using a private account for political purposes "in a bid to circumvent public information laws,"[3] according to reporter Brian Prince in an article on eWeek.com.

In the early years, it was much more difficult to break into a computer system, and so those who were able to do so were

"White hat" hackers broke into Alaskan Governor Sarah Palin's computer account in an attempt to prove that she was using a private account for political purposes.

Famous Teenage Hackers

In the early days of hacking—as, to a certain extent, it still is today—many young people viewed electronic break-ins as glamorous, because it takes a lot of skill. Some hackers even became celebrities, of a sort, to the online community of computer geeks who shared their stories. These teens and twenty-somethings were attracted to computer technology; it was a skill many picked up easily compared to their parents to whom the technology was more foreign. It was a way for these young hackers to bond with and compete against each other. At first, much of what they did was benign. Hackers would simply want to see if they could get inside a computer system; they did not try to damage it or steal information. But the dark side of hacking—called cracking—would change that.

In the 1980s some of these lawbreakers became legends in their own time. Kevin Mitnick, for example, accessed the U.S. government's North American Aerospace Defense Command system in 1982, when he was only seventeen years old. His actions alarmed the government and actually had a positive side effect: Computer security was improved to help prevent foreign spies from repeating what Mitnick accomplished. Mitnick, who spent a number of years in prison for his crime, as well as for a number of cases of computer and wire fraud, would later hack into the Department of Motor Vehicles system and the computers at the companies MCI and Digital Equipment.

Jonathan James, another teenage hacker who went by the name c0mrade, broke into the National Aeronautics and Space Administration (NASA) system in June 1999. James was sixteen years old at the time. While in the NASA system, he downloaded the source code for the International Space Station. With this information, James could have altered life support systems on the space station and killed astronauts (though he did not). The break-in caused NASA to shut down the system, and repairs cost about $40,000.

His crime cost James his freedom, but because he was still a minor, he only served six months under house arrest followed by probation.

admired by other programmers. The best hackers were pro-
claimed to be "gurus" or "wizards." White hats who turn to
criminal activities are called "crackers" or "black hats."

Over time, the programs written by such skilled people
made their way onto the Internet through message boards,
chat rooms, and Web sites. It became easier to find samples
of computer coding that could be copied and then used to
hack into databases and servers without being particularly well
versed in writing code. People who are relatively unskilled in
programming and simply find and reuse code are referred to
as "script kiddies."

Today a large social community has evolved around hackers.
There are even hacker conferences, such as DEFCON, HOPE,
and the Black Hat convention, and magazines, including *2600
Magazine.*

Sophisticated Criminals, Terrorists, and Espionage

The Internet is increasingly being used by dangerous criminals,
and their crimes are becoming very costly. In 2001 Wilson Tang
and Geoffrey Osowski were caught stealing stock shares from
their employer, Cisco Systems. They hacked into the company's
system and put $8 million worth of shares in their names. They
were each sentenced to nearly three years in prison.

While crimes committed within companies still occur,
Internet fraud has become a more common phenomenon.
Groups such as the mafia have gotten into the game; for
example, organized criminals have set up gambling Web sites
that are based overseas (to avoid U.S. regulations and taxes)
but easily accessed anywhere in the world. Web surfers who
play on these casino sites quickly find themselves losing money
gambling and having their credit card information stolen.

Another venue for computer crime is the online auction.
Sites such as the popular eBay can be a home to inscrutable
dealers who offer goods at auction. Once someone wins an
auction and sends money to the seller, the buyer either does

جيش انصار السنة
The Army of Ansar Alsunnah

Terrorists such as the group the Army of Ansar Alsunnah use the Internet to promote their beliefs, encourage violence, and boast of their attacks.

not receive the correct item or does not receive anything at all. Companies like eBay try hard to block such scammers from their sites, but some sites have become so large that patrolling them is very challenging.

On an international level, the Internet also has become a useful tool, not only for thieves but also for the sharing of information. In 2007 MI5 (the United Kingdom government's security service) warned "that British firms doing business in China are being targeted by the Chinese army, which is using the internet to steal confidential information to benefit Chinese companies."[4] The Chinese army had designed software, the MI5 stated, that allowed them to infiltrate foreign companies and take technological and other useful data.

Many Crimes Go Unreported

The full extent of cybercrime of any type is not fully known. Part of the problem comes from the fact that many victims do not report such crimes. This is particularly true of spam, in which computer users are inundated with unwanted e-mails that try to get them to purchase, for example, discount prescription drugs, or visit a Web site that will cause a virus to download to their hard drive. Today people receive so many spam e-mails that most people just delete them and do not report them to the authorities. People who wander into an illegal Web site by accident (or on purpose) also are unlikely to report it to the authorities.

Data gathering on cybercrime also is a challenge because, as Wall states, "information about reported victimization does not flow through a single portal such as the police in the same way as does reporting of street and related crime."[5] Wall notes that there have been a number of academic studies on the phenomenon of cybercrime, but as yet there is no consensus on the data; indeed, experts have not even agreed on the best way to measure the extent of cybercrime.

"International estimates indicate that cybercrime costs approximately $50 billion annually,"[6] according to writer Chris Hale in the book, *Does the Internet Increase the Risk of Crime?* In 2002, 90 percent of those responding to the U.S. Computer Crime and Security Survey reported experiencing security issues in which their computers or networks had been invaded by unauthorized hackers. Most of those reporting in the survey were businesses, as well as a few private computer users. Costs can include damage to computers and networks and the subsequent loss of work time, theft of corporate and private records, theft of intellectual property (including loss of sales from stolen music and video productions), and the costs resulting from identity theft, including legal fees to correct the problem. None of these figures, however, includes the human costs, such as the emotional pain and suffering caused by cybercrime.

Computer Forensics

The tools that are used to capture cybercriminals are useful for Internet and other computer crimes and for more traditional crimes for which lawbreakers happen to use computers and other electronic devices. For example, someone carrying out a more traditional crime, such as mail fraud using letters sent to private residents, may keep track of his or her records on a computer; or, a child pornographer who takes pictures using a digital camera may save the images on a hard drive. In such instances, computer forensics can prove to be just as useful as they are for cybercrimes.

Computer forensic specialists are similar in many ways to traditional crime-scene investigators; they just use more electronic technology to do their jobs. In fact, many computer forensics detectives began their careers as traditional detectives. These forensic specialists are usually part of a cybercrime unit that includes other team members from a law enforcement agency. Working together, they follow procedures for solving a crime that are similar to any other type of investigation. Their mission is to identify and apprehend the suspect, gather and analyze the evidence, and build a case.

CHAPTER 2

The Chase Through Cyberspace

The first step in solving a cybercrime is to track down the criminals responsible. This would be impossible for the investigators without the crimes being reported by a victim or victims. Some victims of cybercrime may not even know to whom to file a complaint, but the usual step is for private citizens to go to their local police. More savvy Internet users alert the Internet Fraud Complaint Center, while corporations might approach a federal agency, such as the Federal Bureau of Investigation (FBI), the Internal Revenue Service (IRS), or the Federal Communications Commission (FCC).

Because the Internet flows through cyberspace internationally, there are many law enforcement organizations that attempt to control crime on both the national and international level. In the United States, cybercrime is a concern addressed by the following agencies:

- The FBI, which has organized the Infrastructure Protection and Computer Intrusion Squad in Washington, D.C., that investigates cybercrime on the national level. The FBI also has created the InfraGuard Web site, a central, secure resource that is used to coordinate information and planning among local and national agencies. The agency runs the Computer Analysis and Response Team (CART) that is staffed by computer forensics specialists.
- The U.S. Department of Justice, which includes several divisions that specifically target various crimes, such as fraud, terrorism, violent crime, theft, and crimes against minors. Its Computer Hacking and Intellectual

*Members of
the Computer
Emergency
Response Team
(CERT) are tasked
with monitoring
the Internet and
responding to
security threats such
as those caused by a
widespread virus.*

Property (CHIP) Unit was first established in northern California, and it is now being deployed in numerous cities across the country.

- The U.S. Department of Defense, which is primarily concerned with terrorism and matters of national security, including those involving cybercrime.

- The U.S. Secret Service, which coordinates its efforts through the Electronic Crime Task Force. The Secret Service, which runs the Electronic Crimes Special Agent Program (ESCAP) uses computer forensics to investigate organized crime, drug cartels, and hacking, and it employs electronic wiretapping in some cases.

- The National Homeland Security Agency, which is primarily concerned with threats involving terrorism, but also is involved in border control and other national issues, such as preventing and investigating cyberspace attacks, as well as coordinating efforts among various law enforcement agencies.

- The IRS, which has a cybercrime resource in its Seized Computer Evidence Recovery (SCER) unit.
- The U.S. Drug Enforcement Administration, which has a computer forensics unit.

There also are a number of nongovernmental regulatory organizations that monitor the Internet, including the Internet Watch Foundation (IWF), the Coalition Against Unsolicited Commercial Email (CAUCE), and the Computer Emergency Response Team (CERT). The IWF is a United Kingdom organization that represents a cooperative effort between Internet service providers (ISPs), police, and the government. CAUCE, which has chapters in North America, Europe, Asia, and elsewhere, is a nonprofit group that focuses on preventing the spread of spam through the Internet. CERT, based at the Carnegie Mellon Software Engineering Institute in Pittsburgh, Pennsylvania, is a collaborative effort between the U.S. government and businesses to fight against viruses and other Internet malware.

All these governmental and nonprofit organizations require the services of computer forensics specialists. There are a number of private companies that provide these services as well.

> **By the Numbers**
>
> **$258.5 MILLION**
>
> **The FBI's 2008 budget to fight cybercrime, a 5.5% increase over 2007**

Experts to the Rescue

Although law enforcement agencies are becoming more savvy about computer forensics, there are times when not enough trained staff is available to tackle technical issues involving a cybercrime. In such instances, detectives and other investigators will turn to outside experts. The supervisor in charge of an investigation also must determine if his or her department has the funds to pay an outside expert and whether coordinating with an outside forensic specialist is possible.

Jurisdiction

Because a cybercriminal can attack a victim in another state or even another country, jurisdiction is a big issue when it comes to computer crimes. The problem has made cooperation between various law enforcement agents all the more important and has made the intervention of federal agencies into crimes that normally would have been under local jurisdiction all the more prevalent.

A lack of law enforcement cooperation between jurisdictions is an ongoing problem that hampers cross-border investigations. The problem is compounded by local politics, budgets, and rivalries between agencies. When foreign agencies become involved in an investigation, the issue of cooperation is made all the more complicated.

Computer crime investigators should always keep legal concerns about jurisdiction in mind when they are working on any case, whether it seems to be a local crime or one that is broader in scope.

In addition to sources such as the FBI's CART team and computer crime units in other agencies, investigators also can consult high-tech corporations, such as Microsoft, Novel, and Cisco. These companies, naturally, hire a wealth of computer experts who are very familiar with their company's systems and thus provide a valuable resource to investigators.

However, criminal justice expert Carl J. Franklin cautions, "Because most private experts are not familiar with the judicial system it is unlikely that the expert will know how to execute a search warrant...or resolve search issues that may affect the evidence's admission in trial. Thus, a private expert should be paired with an experienced agent every step of the way."[7]

Increasingly common is the assistance that law enforcement gets—usually unsolicited—from cybersleuths. These are private individuals with technical expertise who gather evidence against cybercriminals and report it to the authorities. Cybersleuths are

Becoming a Network Security Systems Manager

Job Description:
A network security manager is responsible for keeping computer networks at a company or other organization safe from external or internal attacks that may damage or destroy valuable data or put that data at risk of theft. This position typically oversees the operations of LAN and WAN networks and other telecommunications systems, such as telephone networks. A network security manager typically has a staff of information technology professionals and is responsible for planning and implementing security strategies.

Education:
A four-year, computer-related degree with an emphasis on security is usually preferred.

Qualifications:
Five or more years of experience are required, including in computer programming and personnel management.

Additional Information:
The network security manager position not only demands strong technical skills but also a thorough knowledge of business and management practices and an ability to react quickly to new and unexpected challenges as technology advances. This person must be prepared to respond to new security threats by creating solutions internally or by outsourcing to a reliable vendor.

Salary:
$62,000 to $100,000 per year

white hats who say they believe that the Internet belongs to the public and that it should be safe for people of all ages to navigate.

New York Times reporter Matt Richtel captured the perspective of one cybersleuth in his article, "In the Pursuit of Cybercriminals, Real Detectives Rely on Amateurs": "'As computer geeks, we felt the Internet belonged to us,' said Kevin Patterson, founder of Ethical Hackers Against Pedophilia, a group that works with law enforcement to track down online child pornographers. 'Just like saying, "You're not going to sell crack on our corner," we don't want you to distribute child pornography on our Internet."'[8]

It was cybersleuths who helped to track down the author of the I Love You virus and who have been particularly active in reporting child pornographers to the authorities. In one 1998 case, Ethical Hackers successfully jammed an online discussion group through which a group of cyberpornographers communicated. By doing this, Ethical Hackers prevented these criminals from warning each other that police were about to raid their homes. Police remain wary about the help of cybersleuths, however, since their methods may at times make evidence inadmissible in court.

Valuable Clues

Cybercriminals are well aware of the risks they take in perpetrating online fraud, carrying out computer attacks, or running sites with illegal content. They know that data about their activities is saved by ISPs and other companies that do business on the Internet. But the government and law enforcement are aware of this, too. That is why laws have been put in place mandating that such information be stored for a certain amount of time. This way, there is an existing record that is easily accessible in case an investigation is needed.

"Recent changes to the Federal Rules of Civil Procedure (FRCP) have moved electronic data front and center for *all* companies. Email and electronic files are specifically cited as discoverable information and must be retained and managed,"[9] according to technology analyst George Crump. Depending on the type of company, different laws apply. For example, publicly traded companies must adhere to the Sarbanes-Oxley Act when storing Internet data records, and health-care providers must adhere to the Health Insurance Portability and Accountability Act regarding electronic health-care data. Such laws make it

Online shoppers' credit card information is stored in company databases, causing some to question the information's vulnerability to hackers.

possible for law enforcement to use subpoenas to extract valuable electronic records for investigations.

There is, however, debate about maintaining credit card transactions in company databases. There have been several cases of hackers cracking department store, bank, and credit card company records to steal credit card numbers or customers' identities. In 2007 security expert Max Ray Butler was arrested by the Secret Service and charged with hacking into computer databases and stealing credit card information, which he then sold to others. He was caught when he sold more than one hundred numbers to a police informant.

In reaction to this, states are passing laws that force companies to delete credit card information after a transaction has been completed, or to take other steps, such as ensuring that electronic transactions are encrypted. This way, no information is left for hackers to find. Businesses have been resistant to such legislation because it involves more work, and more money, on their part to ensure the confidentiality of their customers' information. For example, in California, where this

31

How ISP Tracking Works

An Internet protocol (IP) address (which is expressed digitally, such as 15.342.7.455) is an extremely valuable tool for cybercrime investigators. This address, which is unique to every computer, includes identifying data such as the town where the computer is located, the ISP for that computer, and the exact coordinates of the house or business.

ISPs maintain a database that records each registered IP address and who registered it. When someone visits a Web site, the site automatically places a cookie tagging the computer user and his or her browsing habits. Detectives can obtain IP addresses through these cookies and then identify who accessed a particular Web site.

Missouri state patrolman Jeff Owen was able to link a woman accused of murder to her victim by tracing an IP address and examining online message boards.

debate has been raging, businesses argue they have imposed their own security procedures. "The problem is that many companies that accept credit and debit cards don't bother complying with the voluntary standards and are only too happy to avoid the costs of doing so," according to a 2008 *Los Angeles Times* article. "California consumers remain vulnerable to hackers, even if their crimes do not reach the scale of the 2005 TJ Maxx/Marshalls breach, which compromised the data of more than 45 million customers."[10]

Unmasking the Suspect

Cybercriminals employ a number of clever strategies to hide their identities and their activities. In the case of online money laundering, sometimes a part of credit card identity theft and fraud, they may hide information in databases maintained in other countries. According to CNN.com, they might convert money into "anonymous Internet-based currencies to conceal or launder their purchases,"[11] as was the case of a recent credit card scheme involving both Americans and Eastern Europeans in which 40 million accounts were stolen from retail store databases. Internet currency includes such services as InternetCash and V-Cash in which people can convert real, physical currency into anonymous, electronic currency before purchasing items and services.

Not only are foreign databases used to hide information, but also Web hosting companies from other nations. This is a frequent strategy of hackers who set up botnets in one country by attacking victim computers from foreign locations.

Computers connected to the Internet use transport control protocol/Internet protocol (TCP/IP) to communicate with each other and with network servers. This standardized protocol makes it possible for the computer to communicate with any hosting network server. Each computer user has a unique IP address, which is registered and includes a user's address, phone number, and name. Hackers and other savvy cybercrooks know this, and so they employ strategies to hide this information by using "IP addresses that cannot be linked to them. Such IP addresses can be obtained by using free ISPs that allow individuals to dial into the Internet without requiring them to identify themselves," explains computer security consultant Eoghan Casey. He adds, "Other ISPs unintentionally provide this type of free, anonymous service when one of their customer's dial-up accounts is stolen and used by the thief to conceal his identity while he commits crimes online.

Internet cafés offer anonymous ISP addresses, an appealing factor to hackers who do not want their activities traced back to them.

Public library terminals and Internet cafés are other popular methods of connecting to the Internet anonymously."[12]

Cybercriminals also can route their Internet traffic through a proxy server (sort of an intermediary between two servers). When this is done, the IP address that is stored on the destination server is that of the proxy server, not the originating IP address. This is a particularly common strategy for criminals using Internet relay chat (IRC) or the instant messaging ICQ chat. Chat rooms are one way that cybercriminals can distribute malware across the Internet.

NCovert, announced at the 2003 Black Hat conference in Las Vegas, Nevada, is a program designed to hide criminals' identities. It "uses spoofing techniques to hide the source of communications and the data that travels over the network," says computer forensics expert Dario Forte. *Spoofing* is a term referring to how a hacker or other cybercriminal hides his or her true identity in an e-mail or Web site. Forte also says, "the technique essentially creates a covert channel for communications by hiding four characters of data in the header's initial sequence number (ISN) field."[13] Thus, IP addresses are hidden effectively from both hackers and legitimate investigators of Web traffic.

Still another strategy for concealing identities is to set up anonymous e-mail or Usenet accounts. Software programs are readily available on the Internet for anyone to encrypt files or create anonymous e-mail accounts. E-mail forgery is a little less effective, as it might fool some recipients, but experts know that e-mails include the imbedded IP information of the real sender's identity.

There is a problem for investigators tracking down information, however, when it comes to the IP addresses. There are two kinds of IP addresses: static (or dedicated) and dynamic (changing). Static IP addresses are the norm for people using e-mail and Web browsers in a fixed location, such as a home or business. Because people are becoming increasingly mobile— accessing the Internet through laptops, smartphones, and other electronic communication devices—ISPs are more routinely assigning users IPs through the dynamic host configuration protocol (DHCP), which gives users a different IP address each time they log into a different network system.

Another challenge for investigators tracking e-mail is that e-mails are routed through the Internet via different paths, depending on Internet traffic. E-mails get addresses attached to them as they travel through cyberspace. These addresses indicate the media access control (MAC) that identifies a network interface card on a server. As an e-mail is routed, these MACs are attached to it and can be read to identify their source. The problem comes when e-mails travel over the Internet, via different routes, and pick up any number of MACs along the way from any possible combination of routing servers. This makes it very difficult for investigators to track e-mails using just MACs as identification.

Reputable Web sites such as eBay, which polices its site to ensure its policies are enforced, must still deal with dishonest users who commit fraud.

Tracking Web Sites

Invaluable partners in the pursuit of cybercriminals are ISPs and other companies that provide online services, such as the online auction site giant eBay. Each user's IP is registered at

an ISP, and this data, in turn, is maintained by the American Registry for Internet Numbers (ARIN), which is accessible by anyone via the WhoIs service at www.whois.net. A subpoena from the court is necessary in order to obtain records from an ISP. Matching information from other sources with data from an ISP can be an effective tool in cornering a suspect.

Auction fraud is an ongoing problem on the Internet, and even though eBay polices its site as best as it can, there are still disreputable dealers who do not deliver promised goods to auction winners. EBay and the Internet Fraud Complaint Center received several tips about one particular online seller. According to Casey:

> to hide his identity, the seller used a Hotmail account for online communications and several mail drops to receive checks. Logs obtained from Hotmail revealed that the seller was accessing the internet through a subsidiary of Uunet. When served with a subpoena, Uunet disclosed the suspect's MSN account and associated address, credit card and telephone numbers."[14]

Investigators combined this information with subpoenaed data from eBay, the suspect's bank, employees who worked at the suspect's mail drop locations, and real estate records that led police to the suspect's secret, alternate address.

Other electronic sources are available to investigators that may even be more useful than ISP data, especially network systems managed by private corporations. According to Casey, corporate networks commonly maintain records in:

> databases, document management systems, time clock systems [useful for establishing times when crimes were committed], and other networked systems that contain information about individuals who use them. Also, private organizations often configure their networks to monitor individuals' activities more than the

public Internet.... Some organizations monitor which Web pages were accessed from computers on their networks. Other organizations even go so far as to analyze the raw traffic [all the unfiltered, unprocessed data that is not automatically flagged by spyware or virus checkers] flowing through their network for signs of suspicious activity.[15]

There also is the Internet Assigned Numbers Authority (IANA), which is a resource that computer forensic specialists can use to find domain name system (DNS) information to track cybercriminals. The DNS is a database maintained by the Internet Corporation for Assigned Names and Numbers (ICANN) that includes information on who registered which Web site, and it includes both the domain name URL (universal resource locator) address (for example, www.samplewebaddress.com) and the numeric address identifier (such as, 122.450.4.5), which is the address that computers use to communicate to each other the location of a Web site. Investigators can use either the URL or the numeric identifier to access a service, such as Network Solutions to discover the owner of the Web site they are seeking information about.

Finally, there are some basic computer commands that can be run that help trace IP addresses. These include the dig -x ip command, the ping ip command, the finger@ip command, and the Trace-route ip command. Dig -x helps trace DNS servers that show the Web sites that are the source of an Internet attack; Ping and finger@ip will indicate if the hacker or the attacking IP is currently online; Trace-route, a tool available on UNIX operating systems, helps investigators trace the path through which the attack came over the Internet.

Discovering the Web address of an ISP can help trace a criminal to his geographical location. According to Franklin,

another reason addresses are important is that they will show the methods used by the computer suspect to commit the acts in question. For instance, in mail scams ... the DNS, URL, or IP addresses are normally faked or run through various cover addresses. It usually takes awhile, but even with simple programs such as ping or Traceroute the investigator can find a surprising number of links back to the suspect. Knowing those addresses, how they are created, and how they are used in the larger system is a key to being able to track the suspect.[16]

While anti–virus software can help capture dangerous e-mails before they do harm, tracking the source of the e-mails can be difficult. Cybercriminals will hide their identities behind telneting, which allows the e-mails to appear as if they came from someone else.

Tracking E-mails

Cybercrooks leave a trail of evidence in cyberspace as they send e-mails through the Internet. It is a trail forensic investigators can follow in addition to Web site traces.

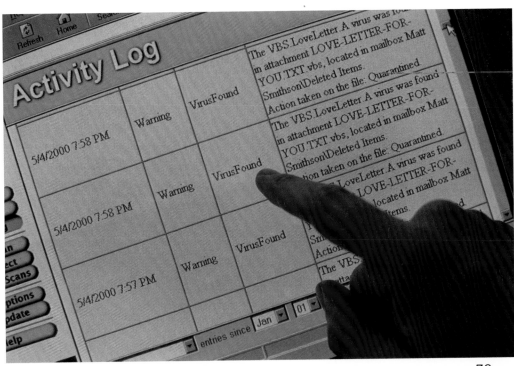

Cybercriminals try to hide their identities when they send spam or e-mails with malware attachments. They do this by using telnet commands to access other computers remotely using the Internet standard e-mail: port 25 (the simple mail transfer protocol, or SMTP). The SMTP does not require user identification, and so hackers can send e-mails without authentic header identifiers. Most e-mail users never see the header identifier code, but disguising or altering this code allows hackers to forge the "From" field so that an e-mail appears to originate from someone other than the criminal.

E-mail headers contain information such as the day and time an e-mail was sent to the recipient, the return path (the e-mail address to which an e-mail is sent if the recipient clicks on "Reply"), the e-mail hosting server's address, and the addresses of any other e-mail servers through which the e-mail traveled (although this information may be altered by the hacker, as well). What cannot be hidden by a hacker, however, is the IP address identifying the originator, and with this information the computer forensic specialist has a solid lead. Investigators can obtain this data by revealing the header code, which can be done in various ways, depending on the software that was used by the sender of the original e-mail.

To discover IP information, investigators may examine the SMTP server log that is maintained by the mail server's hosting company. Server logs maintain data about e-mails as well, including originating IPs and message dates. According to Franklin, "in practice the server log is actually a better source of details than the message header, and the investigator should determine as soon as possible whether the logs will be needed. If they are needed the first step in preserving them is to gain cooperation from the ISP or other server host."[17]

Trying to identify a cybercriminal by tracing his or her activities on the Internet is comparable to narrowing down suspects in a traditional crime. It is just the first step in a long process toward solving the case.

CHAPTER 3

Trapping the Cybercriminal

Solving a cybercrime case takes more than just identifying a criminal who uses computers to attack victims. The case needs to be developed in a number of ways, including evidence gathering and analysis. Once law enforcement has a good idea of who a suspect might be, it is time to figure out how best to trap the person perpetrating the illegal activities. There are a number of ways to capture a cybercriminal in virtual space, including sniffers, keyboard tapping, word bugs, cookies, baiting, and honeypots.

Sniffers and Snoopers

One method used to capture cybercriminals is surveillance through various software programs. Just as with traditional surveillance methods (video tapes, telephone wiretaps), investigators typically need a warrant before monitoring a suspect's computer. Exceptions to this rule might be cases involving national security, which are exempt from the need for advanced warrants thanks to the passage of the 2001 Patriot Act.

There is a wide range of computer programs, used both by law enforcement and private citizens, for snooping on other people's computer use. Programs called sniffers are employed for both legal and illegal purposes. A sniffer program can monitor any kind of traffic (e-mail, file downloads, etc.) entering or leaving a computer that is attached to a network. Companies might use sniffer programs to monitor employee behavior; cybercriminals can use them to record and steal personal data; and law enforcement agencies use sniffers to discover criminal behavior.

Because of the way computers work when attached to a network, a sniffer can detect the information transmitted

Rashid G. NURGALIYEV   Yury Ya. CHAIKA

Ministers from the Group of Eight countries met in 2006 and agreed to cooperate on laws and other measures intended to combat cybercrime.

between them. As network security consultant Matthew Tanase explains:

> Most PCs ... are on a Local Area Network (LAN), meaning they share a connection with several other computers. If the network is not switched (a switch is a device that filters and forwards packets of information between segments of the LAN), the traffic destined for any machine on a segment is broadcast to every machine on that segment. This means that a computer actually sees the data traveling to and from each of its neighbors, but ignores it, unless otherwise instructed.[18]

Sniffers tell network interface cards (NICs) in a network server that the instruction to ignore data traffic from other computers should be turned off. Thus, someone connected to that network and using a sniffer can now see everything traveling through the network. Sniffers also can detect the type of protocol being used (such as e-mail or Web browsing protocols); therefore, the program can not only read the content, but also the information about the source of the data that was generated.

A particularly useful sniffer program used by some computer forensics specialists is the tcpdump utility. Originally, this program was written to analyze data on UNIX systems, but it also is useful in examining network systems, including those running Linux and Solaris operating systems, for data that has been hacked into. Tcpdump captures so many packets of information, however, that it should be used in concert with sifter tools that help pull out the most relevant data.

Network administrators can use sniffer programs legitimately to gather data about Internet usage at, for example, a corporate location. The bad news is that, if investigators can use sniffers to discover Internet activity, so can cybercriminals. Sniffit, for instance, is a readily obtained program that reads unencrypted information traveling through cyberspace. While not overly sophisticated, the program can still capture important data such as passwords and user IDs.

By the Numbers

17

Percentage of companies (with more than 100 employees) that have spyware on their network

Tapping into Typing

A much more direct means of gathering data from a computer is actually monitoring and recording what a person is typing on the keyboard. Many private citizens are already aware of software—such as the K16 Parental Monitoring Software—that allows them to observe the computer activity of, for example, their children. These programs have stealth settings so that the person whose activities are being recorded is not aware that the program has been installed. The keystroke logger (also called keylogger or keystroke grabber) software then creates

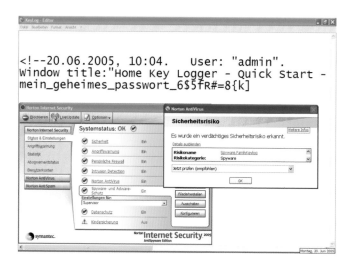

This screenshot depicts a log report in German from a keystroke grabber program. The program is designed to capture keystrokes on a computer and secretly provide the information to someone else, such as an employer or an investigator.

a report that can be secretly e-mailed to a specific recipient. When lawbreakers use increasingly sophisticated encryption methods to conceal the data they are gathering or transmitting, keyloggers can be a useful tool to obtain the information investigators need directly.

The first known case of law enforcement using a keylogger program was in 1999, when Nicodemo Scarfo Jr., a mob boss in New Jersey, was arrested on loan sharking charges. The FBI had obtained a court order to enter Scarfo's home in Belleville and install a keystroke logger, as well as other detection software, onto his computer. This allowed the FBI to learn Scarfo's passwords and access data he had been hiding in his electronic files.

At the time the FBI was able to circumvent legal questions because President Bill Clinton's administration had worked to change federal laws, allowing more leeway for "black bag" jobs (investigations that include breaking into and entering a suspect's home or business).

Since the terrorists attacks of September 11, 2001, federal laws have been revised even more to allow such searches. In a 2007 case, the U.S. Drug Enforcement Agency was able to use a keylogger program called Magic Lantern to hack into the computer of a drug dealer who was manufacturing the illicit drug Ecstasy.

Word Bugs

Investigators may also use word bugs to trace documents. This is a feature that is not commonly understood by most computer users. The word processing program Microsoft Word offers the ability to attach snooping bugs to documents so they can be tracked. The Microsoft Corporation added this feature beginning with Word 97, with the intention that it could be used to prevent copyright and confidentiality violations of important documents. The snooping bugs also are attachable to other Microsoft program files, such as the presentation software PowerPoint and the spreadsheet software Excel.

Microsoft bugs work by attaching an image file to a document. This image can be as obvious as a full-color photograph or as subtle as a one-by-one, clear-colored pixel that is invisible

How Do Cookies Work?

Cookies, also called Web cookies or HTTP cookies, are packets of text information that contain information about a computer user's machine. When a Web surfer visits a site on the Internet, the site transmits a cookie to the visitor's computer, where it is stored. Each time the visitor returns to that site, the cookie identifies him or her as someone who has been to the site before. This is useful for features such as online forms and shopping carts, where data such as names and addresses can be automatically filled in because the information is already stored.

While cookies do not spread viruses or other malware, as some people falsely believe, there can be some risks, especially if a person is on a shared computer. If a Web surfer enters personal data at a site, then the other people who share that computer could potentially visit the same site and learn the first Web surfer's personal information. Also, privacy advocates worry that some Web site companies may collect data from their visitors and then sell this data to others, thus encouraging spam e-mail.

to the eye. The image can then be linked to a Web site, which is then traceable back to the document through the use of cookies.

In computer forensics, this feature comes in handy during investigations involving cases such as stolen proprietary company information and industrial espionage. If a file in Word, Excel, or PowerPoint is tagged with one of these bugs connected to a URL, then each time the file is opened, a record is made. The URL to which it is linked then enters the information into a Web log, which would identify the host server where the document was accessed. This fairly simple technology also could potentially be used on music and video files to track illegally copied songs and movies.

Carnivore and Echelon

More complicated technologies have been developed by the government to snag cybercrooks. Carnivore, for one, was developed by the FBI to monitor Internet activity. First developed during President Clinton's administration, Carnivore worked using Windows operating systems and must be physically installed onto a network computer (such as a company's LAN or an ISP server). Once the Carnivore user was granted administrator rights to the network, he or she had a powerful tool. "For instance, he or she can access the content of all communications and change and edit files at will. What is more, anyone logged in as administrator can hide any evidence of the activity,"[19] according to John R. Vacca in his book, *Computer Forensics: Computer Crime Scene Investigation*. Thus, it was possible for someone who hacked into a system to tamper with evidence, plant false leads, or extract *confidential* information for bribery, extortion, fraud, and so on.

Carnivore was a government secret until 2000, when Congress called for an investigation into its use. The program brought up the serious question of privacy; also, the methods used to obtain data using Carnivore might not have been admissible in a court of law, and technical issues with the software

put it in jeopardy of being hacked into by outside crackers. Nevertheless, the power of this software program made it an irresistible tool for law enforcement for several years.

Using a program called Echelon, federal officials also have taken advantage of the international interconnectedness of the Internet to monitor e-mails from other countries, as well as telephone conversations, faxes, and other communications transmitted via satellite. Echelon is overseen by the National Security Agency, and it has been the subject of criticism from other nations who claim it violates people's rights and can be used for corporate espionage, such as stealing trade secrets. But according to Vacca, "charges cited are mostly old, well-known cases: In 1994, U.S. intelligence discovered that French companies were offering bribes to Saudi Arabia and Brazil for multibillion-dollar contracts. Washington complained, and U.S. firms got the deals."[20] Since then, furor over the use of Echelon has subsided somewhat after many U.S. assurances to the international community that it is not using Echelon for its own commercial advantage.

The National Security Agency oversees the Echelon program, which is run out of several sites around the world. Echelon is designed to capture and analyze electronic communications for potential security issues.

47

Taking the Web Bait

Surveillance of the Internet and other computer networks is a passive form of collecting data that can be used for criminal investigations. Another method is to actually lure cybercriminals into a trap. Lawbreakers themselves use similar strategies to lure the unsuspecting into Web site scams. In a practice called phishing (pronounced "fishing"), they can, for instance, create bogus sites that attract people for one reason or another.

Becoming a Computer Forensic Specialist

Job Description:
A computer forensic specialist uses a wide variety of software tools to locate, extract, preserve, and analyze data on a computer's hard drive or a network server. This position is found in law enforcement, the government, and corporations. A computer forensic specialist can be a full-time employee or a freelancer who has been contracted for a specific project.

Education:
A number of colleges now offer four-year degrees in computer forensics, cybercrime, and computer security. It is important to get at least a bachelor's degree, and master's degrees are often preferred.

Qualifications:
Training should begin with an internship. Many specialists started, too, with a background in the military or at a police department, but today entry-level positions are available after graduating college, as well.

Additional Information:
Computer forensic specialists also are called digital forensics detectives and digital media analysts.

Salary:
$50,000 to $100,000 per year

An example is a Web site that mimics the appearance of a real bank. E-mail messages are sent out to the bank's customers prompting the receiver to click a link to the phony bank site. They are then asked to input important data, such as credit card information, which the cybercriminal then collects. Other examples include illegal gambling or pornography sites that prompt visitors to input personal information.

The same strategy also is used by law enforcement agencies. For instance, law enforcement may create a Web site designed to attract people who are interested in purchasing illegal weapons. When someone enters the site, he or she is offered several chances to opt out of accessing the site's information. For example, the first page of the site could explain what the content is and then ask the site visitor if he or she wishes to proceed by clicking an "enter" button. Several more Web pages may give the site visitor other chances to leave the site without getting into trouble, but if that person repeatedly provides personal information and a willingness to participate in the site's illegal activity, he or she eventually comes to a "gotcha" page that states the site is run by a law enforcement agency and that the visitor's activities have been monitored.

Dipping into the Honeypot

Even more sophisticated than creating a mock Web site is the practice of honeypotting and creating honeynets. A honeypot is any system—whether a computer, a Web space, or even a set of computer files and folders—that mimics a system that a hacker would want to break into. It is a deliberate set up that is intended for an outside hacker to crack into; it records the hacker's break-in methods for later analysis by a computer forensic specialist. Such entrapment, when conducted by private individuals or companies, can be interpreted as breaking the Federal Wiretap Act and therefore should be limited to law enforcement agencies. Honeypotting is a time-consuming method that would not likely be implemented at a crime scene, but rather would be used for a long-term investigation.

Lance Spitzner founded the Honeynet Project, one of the leading efforts to monitor the black hat hacker community.

According to the Honeynet Project, a nonprofit research organization dedicated to making the Internet a safer place:

a honeynet is a type of honeypot. Specifically, it is a high-interaction honeypot designed to capture extensive information on threats. High-interaction means a honeynet provides real systems, applications, and services for attackers to interact with, as opposed to low-interaction honeypots…which provide emulated services and operating systems. It is through this extensive interaction we gain information on threats, both external and internal to an organization. What makes a honeynet different from most honeypots is that it is a network of real computers for attackers to interact with. These victim systems (honeypots within the honeynet) can be any type of system, service, or information you want to provide.[21]

By the Numbers

70

Percentage of American workers who use wireless Internet connections at least part of the time

Because they are designed to be intentionally attacked, honeypots and honeynets can be risky when installed on LANs and other networks. To help protect the network, programs are installed that limit what a hacker can do to alter or extract network files and programs.

Wireless Surveillance

The development of wireless networks created yet another challenge for law enforcement. Networks are increasingly abandoning physical connections of cables and phone lines for the more liberating wireless connection. Wireless networks have the advantage of not being burdened by clumsy cords, but they can be particularly vulnerable to hackers and crackers. They are easily accessed because hackers do not need a physical connection to enter a wireless network; they just need to be in range of the transmitting signal. Also, data transferred between computers on a wireless network tends to be poorly encrypted compared to wired networks. According to an article in *USA Today*, a 2007 survey conducted by the security company AirDefense studied more than three thousand U.S. retail stores and found that 25 percent of them "were using an outdated encryption method called Wireless Equivalent Privacy that AirDefense said is easily cracked by thieves using widely available tools."[22]

Because wireless communication is still relatively new, a standardization of protocols has not been established yet, and so there is often a lack of data encryption in such communications. Also, defense mechanisms against viruses have not been put into place in some of the wireless software that is currently available. This makes smartphones, such as BlackBerry and iPhone more susceptible to electronic assaults, including phishing, trojans, and distributed denial of service (DDoS) attacks. As these electronics become more sophisticated and offer more capabilities, the problem is only compounded.

Electronic Communications Privacy Act

A number of federal laws have been passed over the years in an attempt to anticipate the potential abuses against personal privacy that electronic surveillance might impose. One of the most important laws is the Electronic Communications Privacy Act of 1986. The act is intended to cover all types of electronic communications, including wired and wireless forms, and provides guidance as to what is and is not allowed when it comes to intercepting, accessing, and reporting data transmitted between private individuals or corporations. The law specifically prohibits government agencies from seizing such data without following proper procedures.

While defenses against such weaknesses are being created—the Computer Emergency Response Team (CERT) is working on classifying DDoS incidents in order to better defend against them—law enforcement can monitor wireless activity. If investigators have physical access and administrative rights to the network being analyzed, they can attach a sniffer that can detect wireless traffic just as with a wired LAN network. Working outside a network, computer forensic specialists can use wireless sniffers, and there are several available programs for this. Programs such as Airsnort and Ethereal not only capture Web traffic but also can debug encryption and generate easily readable reports in a graphics user interface format.

Going Undercover Online

Not all cybersleuthing involves computer programming. Sometimes, more traditional methods are just as effective. A time-proven strategy that works particularly well in capturing

The Internet allows investigators such as those on New Jersey's Operation Guardian to easily go undercover to capture individuals engaged in Internet crimes such as cyberbullying or child pornography.

potential sex offenders and cyberbullies is for law enforcement to go undercover. This takes advantage of the fact that it is simple to assume a false identity while using chat rooms; instant messaging; social sites, such as Facebook; or e-mail. A law enforcement agent poses, for example, as an underage teen or child and then allows a suspect to engage in an online dialogue. Thinking that the other person online is really a child, the cyberbully or molester will allow himself to reveal information that is crucial to an investigation. The criminal might even set up a face-to-face meeting with the "child" and thus be easily captured by police.

In a 2002 undercover case, a police officer in Palm Beach, Florida, posed as a fourteen-year-old boy in an America Online chat room. A priest in the area began sending him sexually explicit messages, and after a number of correspondences had been sent, the police accused the priest of soliciting sex from a minor. In another case in 2008, Greenville, North Carolina, police arrested a fifty-six-year-old man who had been talking to a police officer in a chat room. The man thought that the officer was a thirteen-year-old girl and asked her to meet him to have sex. These are just two of the many cases for which law enforcement has used undercover Internet communications to capture criminals.

CHAPTER 4

Gathering the Evidence

O nce investigators are ready to close in and arrest a cyber-crook, they need to make sure that they will have enough evidence to make the case against the suspect in court. The amount of data available from tracing a lawbreaker through cyberspace is fairly limited, although it is a vital start. The original computer used by the perpetrator provides a wealth of information. Some of this data, if not deleted by the computer user, is easily found in the Web browser history and temporary Internet files. Most cybercriminals, though, are savvy enough to try and delete this information. Fortunately, incriminating files might still be saved in places such as the computer's registry or Web site connection logs that are less easily removed. Even files that have been deleted leave fragments behind that can be pieced together.

While cybercrime might be a new crime for law enforcement, many of the basic procedures in obtaining evidence for a conviction still apply. Investigators who have identified possible suspects in a computer crime will often desire two types of evidence: physical evidence and data records. Physical evidence may include computers and on-site servers, but other evidence may be gathered at a scene, such as fingerprints; personal records, such as checkbooks and bills; and statements from witnesses. Data records may include telephone records and information from Internet service provider (ISP) servers.

Obtaining Search Warrants

As with any crime, the law requires that police and other government agents have probable cause in order to obtain a search warrant. To convince a judge that a warrant is justified,

A police officer carries computer equipment from the home of a suspect. Obtaining the equipment used by a criminal can provide law enforcement with a wealth of information that they are unable to gather in cyberspace.

investigators need to provide specific information about the evidence they are seeking. This includes a detailed report on the type and number of computers that they plan to search, what kinds of storage devices will be obtained, and other specifics about hardware and software. They also need to make a convincing argument that they should be allowed to seize these items.

According to computer forensics expert Marjie T. Britz:

By the Numbers

160 GIGABYTES

Average amount of data collected during a cybercrime investigation

as warrants provide a cornucopia of legal issues at the trial level, the importance of warrant preparation cannot be overstated. Thus, any warrant application should be reviewed by as many specialists (i.e., computer investigators, legal counsel, etc.) as possible prior to magistrate approval. This…ensures that all equipment, media, and incidentals which may prove evidentiary are included.[23]

A women reviews a search warrant where her computer will be searched. The warrant must provide details on the type and number of computers that will be searched, what kinds of storage devices will be obtained, and other specifics about hardware and software.

Booby-Trapped Computers

The job of a computer forensic specialist can include some unpleasant surprises. It is expected during an investigation that criminals will have tried to delete computer evidence or hide it behind passwords, but occasionally they set booby-traps as well.

A computer booby-trap is a program that detects when a computer is being accessed by someone other than the main user. This can be done by requiring the user to press certain keys or clicking specific desktop icons after booting up a computer, and, if this is not done, a program will launch that will start deleting, or at least damaging, any incriminating data stored on the computer and any disks in it.

Warrants for computer crimes are unique in that typical search warrants only let investigators search for a computer itself; they do not allow police and forensics specialists to search the actual files within a computer. For this reason, secondary or multiple warrants are required for computer crimes. Such warrants allow detectives to broaden their search should they discover additional evidence of an incriminating nature. For example, a detective searching a computer for files relating to a drug case might find evidence of child pornography and wish to collect this evidence as well. Having a secondary warrant on hand allows the investigator to also seize the pornography.

A special no-knock warrant may be obtained in some computer investigations, such as when the case involves a potentially violent criminal or when there is a strong risk that the evidence might be destroyed. Judges who sign this type of warrant allow law enforcement to enter a private home or business without knocking or ringing the bell first so they can take the occupants by surprise.

Special Justification for Searches

Suspects in a criminal investigation are protected from unreasonable searches and seizures by the Fourth Amendment of the U.S. Constitution. This is why warrants are needed. However, there are a number of exceptions to this rule. A sneak-and-peek warrant, recently allowed by the Patriot Act, allows law enforcement to search without notifying the owner if a court believes that forewarning might cause evidence tampering, endangerment to an individual, or other risks to the case.

Investigators also may examine on-site evidence if they are given consent by a third party. This is especially useful in the case of computers that are accessed by more than one user, whether at a home or a private business. For example, a wife or husband can permit police to search a computer used by a spouse; parents can permit detectives to examine a child's computer if he or she is under eighteen years of age; and businesses can allow employee computers to be searched.

Another useful exception is when a network system administrator provides law enforcement with access to files on a server. According to the U.S. Department of Justice:

> as a practical matter, the primary barrier to searching a network account pursuant to a system administrator's consent is statutory, not constitutional. System administrators typically serve as agents of 'provider[s] of electronic communication service' under the Electronic Communications Privacy Act (ECPA).... ECPA regulates law enforcement efforts to obtain the consent of a system administrator to search an individual's account.... Accordingly, any attempt to obtain a system administrator's consent to search an account must comply with ECPA.[24]

Organizing an Investigation

Once detectives obtain a warrant, it is time to pull together a team of computer forensic specialists and other crime-scene investigators to examine and collect the evidence

National Scope of Operation
29 STATES

CALIFORNIA	ALASKA	MONTANA	OKLAHOMA	MISSOURI	WISCONSIN	OHIO	FLORIDA	MARYLAND
OREGON	NEVADA	COLORADO	KANSAS	TEXAS	ILLINOIS	INDIANA	NO. CAROLINA	PENNSYLVANIA
WASHINGTON	UTAH	IDAHO	NEBRASKA	LOUISIANA	MICHIGAN	TENNESSEE	VIRGINIA	RHODE ISLAND
			NEW YORK		NEW JERSEY			

A map of the United States displays the scope of a cyber-sting targeting child pornography. More than two hundred suspects in twenty-nine states were identified during the investigation.

on-site, as well as to interview witnesses and record images of the site. A well-balanced investigative team should include a physical search team to identify and properly mark evidence; a seizure team that carefully gathers the evidence and should be comprised only of computer forensic experts; a sketch and photo team that records what the site looks like; an interview and interrogation team to talk to witnesses and suspects; security and arrest teams to provide on-site security, protection, and arrest support; and finally a case supervisor who oversees the complete operation. The investigative team, therefore, should have computer forensic experts, crime-scene investigators, police officers, detectives, and a supervisor.

Once assembled, the investigative team will require tools to carry out the on-site search. Along with the typical materials needed for any crime-scene investigation, such as photography equipment, storage containers for evidence, wrenches, screwdrivers, hammers and nails, scissors and wire cutters, flashlights, and labels, the computer forensics specialists will need special electronic equipment and software.

Among the tools required for a cybercrime investigation are computer hardware and software, computer peripherals,

Preparing Computer Evidence

To ensure that no evidence is lost or missed during a computer crime investigation, law enforcement personnel follow a set of established procedures. Presenting these procedures in court also ensures that a judge and jury will be convinced that the evidence obtained applies to the case fairly. Typical procedures are:

1 To locate the evidence and make a complete list of computer hardware and software seized.

2 To sort the evidence according to what is considered to be the most relevant and admissible and what is likely to be irrelevant.

3 To determine what is the most volatile computer system and collect this data first. This includes temporary file systems, registries, portable disk drives, and caches.

4 To collect the evidence using pretested software tools.

5 To record any variations in the systems' clock settings to make sure that time lines are accurately established. Note whether local time or Coordinated Universal Time (sometimes called Greenwich Mean Time) is used.

6 To document every step that is taken. Label all physical evidence and make notes about the contents and software used relevant to electronic data.

D. Brezinski and T. Killalea, "Guidelines for Evidence Collection and Archiving," The RFC Archive, http://www.rfc-archive.org/getrfc.php?rfc=3227, February 1, 2002.

cables, cords, power strips, surge protectors, and backup disks. Computer forensic specialists use a wide variety of software for their investigations, including imaging software, which duplicates data from a hard drive; antivirus software to protect the investigators' computers; password cracking software; recovery and viewer software that allows detectives to locate suspect information; and text and hex editors that allow investigators to search text and image files to find relevant text and photographs, especially those that may have been altered to hide them from the police.

On-Site Evidence Gathering

When conducting on-site investigations, detectives and forensic specialists need to keep in mind several issues, including safety, integrity of evidence, and legal considerations, or else their cases may be thrown out of court.

Law enforcement agents understand that, even though they are investigating a computer crime, the individuals involved may be just as dangerous as murder or drug suspects. They may be armed, so law enforcement approaches crime sites with extreme caution. Upon arrival at a crime scene, the suspects are isolated, and possibly arrested, and computers and related equipment are immediately located, identified, and guarded by a police officer to prevent tampering.

Then recording of evidence begins. The first step is to record any readily visible evidence. This includes all computers and any information displayed on their monitors, as well as any printouts easily located on desks, tables, and elsewhere. It is important to note the location of the power source for the computers and servers and to ensure that this source is not cut off, as this can result in a loss of unsaved data that could be valuable to the investigation. This also applies to other electronics, such as cell phones; iPods; personal digital assistants (PDAs); and even computer game systems, like Xbox and Wii; and car navigation systems that record where suspects have traveled.

Non-computer-related evidence at the scene is important, too. Criminals may leave behind clues ranging from written documents and sticky notes, to fingerprints, articles of clothing, and DNA-related evidence, such as strands of hair. These must all be recorded and thoroughly documented.

Freezing the Scene

Freezing the scene is a basic form of evidence collection conducted at the crime scene. It is the recording of data on a seized computer, including any compromised and encrypted data, using imaging software. A lot of data on a computer is saved only temporarily and is lost when a computer is turned off. Therefore, it is essential not to turn off a seized computer at the scene before an investigation has been thoroughly completed. Freezing records data such as that found in temporary Internet file folders, browser histories, address resolution protocol caches (data preserving files shared between networks and ISPs), passwords, credit card information, instant message logs, media history logs, and logs of recently opened files.

Viewer programs may be used by investigators to gain a quick look into the files that are saved on a computer, but the actual preservation of the data is captured by imaging software. Imaging is like taking a photograph of the inside workings of a computer, allowing forensics specialists to see all the files and code exactly as the last user left them.

When files are deleted or otherwise altered on a computer, they leave behind evidence in the form of fragments of code that have not been completely eliminated. If a cybercriminal has not physically destroyed a hard drive, or used a disk-wiping program that deletes the drive of everything, there will always be evidence of data left behind.

Various software tools can be used to detect fragments of code, and it is important that the forensic specialist be careful not to accidentally alter the contents of a suspect hard drive. "The copied data that an examiner uses to reach conclusions are inexorably linked to the validity of the collected image,"[25] according to Curt Bryson and Scott Stevens in the *Handbook of Computer Crime Investigation: Forensic Tools and Technology.* Imaging software tools, therefore, need to be tested before an examination of a suspect's hard drive to ensure they are functioning correctly.

Imaging Software

There are a number of programs available for imaging computer data. EnCase, created in 1998 by Guidance Software, is one of the most frequently used programs. EnCase is designed only for use on personal computers (PCs), not Macintoshes, but since PCs are used by the majority of people, EnCase is a handy tool for computer forensic specialists.

EnCase looks for errors and changes in files. The program can be run to check hard drives and peripheral drives, such as CD-ROMs, DVDs, flashcards, and zip disks.

EnCase not only images the files, but also analyzes them, checking for and recovering deleted files (such as records of Web browsing and Usenet newsgroups) and user logs, for example. There has been some criticism of EnCase because its ability to check if files have been altered is considered by some experts to not be completely free of security issues. There are ways Encase can be fooled, leading investigators to believe that files have not been altered. Also, because EnCase is a forensics tool that is well known to computer criminals, skilled and unscrupulous programmers have worked to create software to help lawbreakers avoid having their files detected by this program.

Despite such potential problems, EnCase remains a very popular program because it can display several types of data analysis in easy-to-view Windows formats. For example, it can display a list of files, present a table of photo images stored on a drive, present a time line of when files were accessed and/or modified, and show all of this in a table format that can be sorted in many useful ways.

Other Recovery Software

Another professional-quality software program is SafeBack, which has been commonly used by law enforcement professionals and the military since the 1990s. It is similar to EnCase in its imaging abilities, but one advantage of SafeBack is that it has both a verify mode, which is a testing mode in which the forensic specialist can test backups on a boot disk, and a copy mode, which makes the actual image of the hard drive.

There are other file-recovery programs, too. Ghost is a program that clones hard drives for recovery. From a forensics point of view, Ghost may be more suitable as a backup program that makes an extra copy of the computer's contents; this is

Data recovery programs can be run on computer hard drives and flash drives to search existing and deleted files.

because when it creates a copy it alters files in ways that may make them unsuitable as trial evidence.

Password Cracking

In addition to deleting or altering data, cybercriminals—like many other computer users—try to safeguard information by creating passwords to protect it. Sometimes basic sleuthing can help investigators locate a password, such as when a suspect has a password written on a piece of paper that is at the scene. If a suspect has not been too imaginative with his or her password, then investigators might be able to guess what it is. For example, many people use their own name or birth location or the name of a friend, loved one, pet, favorite book, movie, or celebrity. Detectives who already know something about the suspect—perhaps through interviews—can occasionally guess a password.

A computer screen displays a password attack in process. An investigator is attempting to access a protected site.

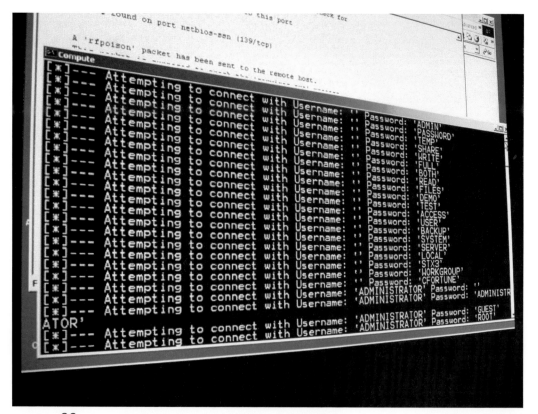

Another option is a program that runs through all the words in the dictionary, one by one, to find the password. However, this will not work if the password contains words and numbers or is a nonsense word.

More often, computer forensic specialists use password-cracking programs to find a password. There are a number of programs available to do this, such as Password Recovery Toolkit. This program can uncover passwords for many of the software programs commonly used today, such as Microsoft Outlook and Word, CCMail, and Quicken. According to Britz, Password Recovery Toolkit "may be used independently or integrated with other forensic software." She also writes, "In addition, it allows for the importation of specialized word lists, and also provides for the exportation of word lists, enabling investigators to use a suspect drive against itself (i.e., by creating a dictionary comprised of every word on the suspect machine including passwords.)"[26]

Passwords, however, may not only be attached to individual files or software programs, but also to the entire hard drive. A hard drive password protects the computer from being booted up by anyone who does not know the password. There are, however, tools and methods available for getting around this security.

COFEE Served the Microsoft Way

A wide variety of software investigative tools that have been created since the 1990s have greatly streamlined the process of computer forensics investigations, which at one time involved the laborious process of searching through lines of digital code. Many of these tools can work together to extract data from a suspect's computer in what can be a rather complicated process. In 2007 Microsoft created a new program to help make forensic work even more efficient. Called the Computer Online Forensic Evidence Extractor (COFEE), the program is offered on a thumb drive that is plugged into the computer under investigation. It combines 150 different commands to extract data without compromising the files. "It also eliminates the need to seize a computer itself, which typically involves disconnecting from a network, turning off the power and potentially losing data. Instead, the investigator can scan for evidence on site,"[27] according to *Seattle Times* reporter Benjamin J. Romano.

Law enforcement agencies in fifteen countries were using COFEE as of 2008, and Microsoft has been distributing it to police and other professionals for free. The logic behind this decision is that Microsoft has a vested interest in keeping lawbreakers off the Internet and electronic devices in general, since they have a majority share of that market.

CHAPTER 5

Making the Case

Computer forensics plays a significant role in cases involving crimes perpetrated using sophisticated technology and, usually, the Internet. It is very important for computer forensics specialists to ensure that data collected from electronic sources supports the charges being made. Professionally preparing the evidence in a case, accurately analyzing the data gathered, and providing testimony in court are all part of proving a cybercrime case.

Preserving Evidence

Just as with physical evidence, electronic evidence can be contaminated. Computer files can be corrupted and this is why file backups and imaging are so important in investigations.

"Originals [of computer evidence] should never be used in forensic examination," warns computer security expert John Vacca, "verified duplicates should be used. This not only ensures that the original data remains clean, but also enables examiners to try more *dangerous*, potentially data-corrupting tests. Of course, any tests done should be done on a clean, isolated host machine."[28]

Good practices in collecting and labeling evidence also must be followed, just as in other, traditional crime-scene investigations. Computer forensics expert Marjie Britz explains:

> Like any scientific evidence, great care must be exercised when collecting and preserving crime scene evidence. The chain of custody and continuity of possession must be maintained at all times for court admissibility. Investigators should adhere to standard operating

procedures for custodial evidence collection—keeping in mind that routinization enhances witness credibility and evidence validity.[29]

All physical evidence at the scene needs to be carefully and accurately labeled, including all computer components, peripherals, memory cards and disks, wires, and cables. Latex gloves should be worn to keep physical evidence, such as fingerprints, from being compromised. Britz warns that computer electronics also can be damaged by dust, static electricity, overly hot temperatures, and even magnetic fields. She writes, "Any type of magnetic field poses a potentially calamitous risk to computer media and hardware. Even low-level magnetic pulses, such as those emitted from car radios and

Just as with other criminal investigations, it is important to properly process and protect evidence in cybercrimes by following the proper chain of custody and continuity. These measures help ensure electronic evidence will be admissible in court.

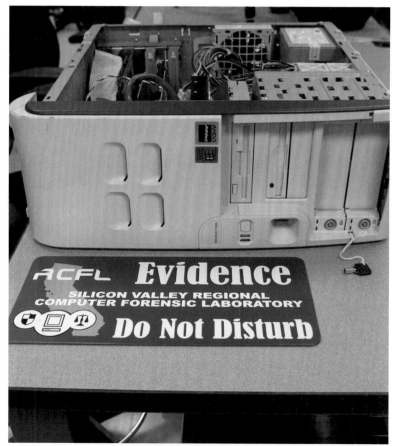

transmitters, create an environment hazardous to computer-related evidence."[30]

Once everything has been properly tagged, computers and storage devices must be kept in a secure location where they will not be accessed by anyone not directly involved in the investigation. Any access to a computer, however well-intentioned, by unauthorized personnel can cause data on the hard drive to be changed and make it unusable in court. Computer forensics specialists run a mathematical authentication program on the computer that verifies that no data has been altered in any way.

There is another issue, too, that is problematic concerning computer evidence. Digital data can decay over time. Court cases, depending on the nature of the crime, can

Preparing Evidence for Court

Ensuring that computer evidence is admissible in court means that law enforcement must follow certain procedures when preparing the data collected for the case. These procedures are:

1. A specific, qualified person should be assigned to monitor all the collected computer crime evidence.

2. Whenever possible, the evidence should be maintained in an untouched, unaltered state. This includes the original files, software, and hardware, and any imaged data.

3. If, for some reason, the evidence must be accessed and examined in a way that could potentially alter it, a competent computer forensics examiner must be present at all times, and he or she must document everything that is done during the examination process and by whom.

4. All evidence recorded must be maintained in such a way that a third party could reproduce what was done and create the same results discovered by the original examiners.

sometimes drag on for many months or even years. Some storage devices, such as CD-ROMs, can begin to decay after one or two years, and this should be kept in mind when storing electronic evidence.

Documenting the Evidence

Just like other types of evidence, computer files and related equipment must be documented. Information that needs to be recorded includes file names, document creation and modification dates, data on fragmented or partially erased files, the names and versions of the software programs in question, whether or not the software is legally licensed, the case number, and the names of law enforcement personnel handling the evidence. Documenting the type of software and the version is particularly important because manufacturers maintain information on known bugs in these programs that could potentially affect the data discovered.

Chain of Custody

As computer evidence travels from the scene of the crime to a crime lab and to a courtroom, it is handled by many law enforcement personnel. This is why it is vital to document thoroughly who has been in contact with the evidence along the way. In his book, *The Investigator's Guide to Computer Crime*, criminal justice expert Carl J. Franklin writes, "When prosecutors present evidence to a court, they must be ready to show that the evidence they offer is the same as that seized by the investigators and if it has changed why or how."[31]

An evidence officer is put in charge of keeping track of this record, including not only who has handled the evidence but also whether or not anything was done to it along the way. The evidence officer also keeps track of notes made about tests conducted and any other comments from investigators pertaining to the evidence.

Analyzing the Evidence

Raw evidence gathering is not the only task of a crime-scene investigator, although it is a key part of the job. Computer forensics specialists are expected to analyze the data they have collected and try to make sense out of it. This includes conducting tests on computer files.

The difference between a traditional investigation and a computer investigation is that in a computer investigation it is much more challenging to trace the sequence of events. With a murder case for instance, a detective may find evidence that can help establish a time line and identify suspects. Evidence, such as footprints, fingerprints, blood or hair samples, or a murder weapon, can assist police in reconstructing what happened. With a computer, however, all that the computer forensics specialist usually has is data on the computer at the time that it was seized. The specialist can only theorize about the original state of the computer and about anything that may have occurred between the time the

Computer forensics specialists must analyze electronic data to build a criminal case against a suspect. Because all computers have security vulnerabilities, some data on a computer may actually misdirect an investigator.

crime was committed and the time the computer was seized.

Computer security expert Brian D. Carrier explains:

If you saved every state and event of the computer (i.e. its history), then you could answer any digital investigation question about it. Unfortunately, a digital investigator will have only the current state of the system or the state when an acquisition was performed. Perhaps he will also have backups of the system, which represent the state of the system at a previous time. He must make inferences about the previous states of the system. For example, given the current state, he must make inferences about what events caused the system to get into that state.[32]

Carrier says that while an investigator can pose questions about the current state of the data on a computer, and even query about data from a past state, he or she cannot discover cause-and-effect relationships. For example, a computer forensics specialist might find a file that indicates a user of the computer visited a gambling site. It is possible, however, that this information was implanted by a computer virus, or someone other than the suspect used the computer.

Educated Assumptions

Analyzing computer evidence is a challenge. Since computer forensic specialists only have the data that was on the computer at the time it was seized to work with, their conclusions based on that data are theories. According to Carrier, the most effective approach is to make educated assumptions. He writes:

> To be a scientific process though, we should be making hypotheses and testing them. We should be stating that we think program X was installed at time Y and test the statement by trying to prove that it was NOT installed. If we can find evidence that it was installed and we cannot show that it was not installed, then we can conclude with an amount of certainty that it was installed. However, digital forensics is not at that point yet because we have no objective way of calculating how confident we are in our conclusions.[33]

Sometimes, in specific cases, such as proving whether a certain software program is capable of generating an output claimed by a defendant, computer forensics is able to answer such questions irrefutably. More involved processes that require a long trail of events are too challenging and require too much data to prove in many cases. What a computer investigator *can*

Vishing for Details

Vishing is a crime similar to phishing, except that it takes advantage of voice over Internet protocols (VoIP). Like phishing, vishing uses social engineering techniques to lure people into a scam. Instead of e-mail, however, vishing uses telephone services available through the Internet. Most people who use this technology trust it more than e-mail because the voice communication is connected to land lines that are more easily traced by phone companies. However, just as with e-mails, spoofing is possible using VoIP, so it is wise to always be suspicious of anyone who is making a request for credit card numbers or other personal information, no matter what technology is used to reach someone.

do is provide informed, possible scenarios using sample data to show how a crime might have been committed.

Daubert Guidelines, which are used to determine admissibility of scientific evidence in court, also should be considered when deciding how to examine data stored on a computer or other electronic device. In *Forensic Computer Crime Investigation,* Fred Cohen writes that the guidelines include questions such as: "(1) Has the procedure or technique been published? (2) Is the procedure generally accepted? (3) Can and has the procedure been tested? (4) What is the error rate for the procedure?"[34]

While still not a perfected science, analyzing digital evidence can still help investigators solve cases.

Establishing Time Lines

As anyone who has watched a crime drama or a real trial on television knows, establishing the times when events occurred is extremely important in proving guilt in many court cases. If, for example, a prosecutor wanted to prove that a suspect was at a bank at a certain time, but a log file on the suspect's computer indicated he was writing a letter to his mother at the time, then the case could suffer a setback.

One might believe that establishing time lines using computers would be fairly simple because all computers include internal clocks, and file directories show when text, graphic, and other files have been saved.

Computer clocks may not always be accurate, however, especially if a user has adjusted the time display; even if the clock is off only by a few minutes, this could be significant in a trial. The internal clock on an individual computer also can be synchronized with a network clock, but then the network clock must be checked for accuracy, too.

It also should be noted which time zone the clock is set for, as it is possible that a computer may have been moved from another time zone. And, different operating system versions perform differently depending on their use, including the

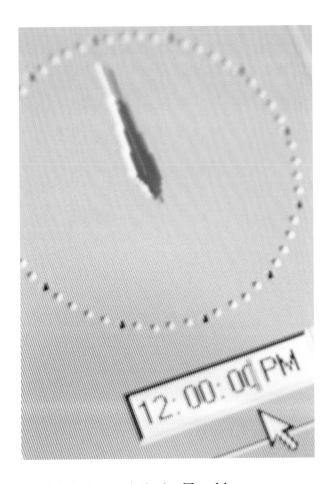

Establishing timelines on computers is difficult since users can manipulate the computer's clock and time zone therefore providing incorrect times for certain activity.

accuracy of their internal clocks. To add even more complexity to the task, the software tools that forensic specialists use also may have variations in how they record file creation and alteration times. This is why it is important that all tools used in a criminal examination be tested, and their performance documented, before their use on evidence.

Software, such as the Stamper, is available that can establish accurate days and times attached to computer files.

Missed or False Evidence

In cases involving computer crime, as in all criminal cases, the possibility of missed or falsified evidence exists. In computer crimes this can be compounded by the complex nature of computer forensics. Computer hard drives and storage devices can

Though evidence found on a computer may be considered to be unreliable, offenders can still be effectively prosecuted. Kevin Poulsen was charged with espionage in 1990 after he hacked into FBI and national security computer systems.

contain so much information in states ranging from whole and uncorrupted to damaged, hidden, and temporary, that there are many ways data can be missed, even by an experienced forensics team. It is even possible that clever cybercriminals have created false evidence on their computers, although this is extremely difficult to do.

Cohen writes, "Just because a computer says so doesn't make it so."[35] In other words, even when investigators have followed all the correct procedures, extracting and preserving evidence from a computer or storage device, the information on a computer is not necessarily true. Cohen explains, "The sources of errors in computers are wide-ranging. From computer viruses that leave pornographic content in computers, to remote control via Trojan horses that allow external users to take over a computer from over the Internet, to just plain lies typed in by human beings, computers are full of wrong information."[36]

Providing Testimony

An unusual aspect of computer evidence is that, in many circumstances, it is considered hearsay by the courts. Hearsay evidence is information that is not based on a witness's personal knowledge. In other words, a witness cannot testify about something he or she heard someone else say. When a computer forensics specialist testifies in court about evidence found within a computer, the computer, in essence, is the real witness. Some leeway is granted in courts for this, however, but this makes the reliability of the expert on the stand all the more important. It is vital that the testimony comes from a source that is as much beyond reproach as possible.

The Future of Cybercrime

Cybercrime has become increasingly common because of advancements in technology. The tools to combat it are the same tools that lawbreakers use, and keeping ahead of the criminals is a constant challenge for law enforcement. A big

Electromagnetic Pulse Bombs

In the science-fiction television series, *Dark Angel*, the United States collapses in the year 2019 after it is attacked by an electromagnetic pulse bomb that destroys all its computer technology. While this scenario may seem far-fetched, it is actually possible to launch a kind of electronic bomb using explosives, not computers.

It was during nuclear testing that scientists first observed that an electromagnetic shockwave through the atmosphere could wreak havoc on electronic communications. The use of copper wiring for telecommunications makes these systems vulnerable to such crude attacks. More recently, as metal wiring is replaced with fiberoptics, the United States has become somewhat less vulnerable to the scenario of a terrorist attack using electromagnetic pulse bombs.

concern of law enforcement is that the Internet has become a repository of information about how to hack into computer networks and commit other cybercrimes, all without the need for sophisticated technical knowledge. Those who wish to perform attacks on individual computers or networks need only find the right illicit software package, download it, and run it in order to perform multiple operations that a few years ago could only be accomplished by knowledgeable programmers.

Search engines such as Google also have become unwitting tools of cybercriminals, who have figured out how to conduct Web searches to locate Web sites that use outdated or vulnerable software and exploit those weaknesses. Furthermore, the Internet is becoming omnipresent in the most unlikely places, such as Web-connected photo frames and kitchen appliances.

Crimes committed by individual lawbreakers are not the only worry. Cybercrime has become an international issue that threatens national security. For example, there are growing concerns about spies using computer technology to steal industrial

and government secrets and about terrorists who are spreading their message of hatred across the Internet.

Information warfare is now a tactic used by terrorists and foreign nations to spread propaganda against the enemy by using high-tech means.

More than one thousand computer hackers gather at the Chaos Communication Camp 2007 in Germany to share software and knowledge.

Partnerships May Offer Solutions

For years the first line of defense against cyberattacks has rested with private citizens and corporations. People who did not use firewalls, antivirus software, and other defenses were responsible for their own victimization by hackers, crackers, and other black hats. More recently, however, the major computer hardware providers, Microsoft and Apple, have come to recognize that it is in their best interest to provide better security for their customers. Microsoft's Vista operating system is a good example of how the company is designing software to include security.

Vista introduced a security application called BitLocker that allows users to not only protect their personal files with a password but also set a password for *all* hard drive contents that lacked such protection before. Next, when Windows 7 was released in the fall of 2009, Microsoft added AppLocker. AppLocker is meant for IT administrators, who can now maintain a list of software applications they wish to "lock" or prevent from running because they are not used, unwanted, or known to be malware.

In 2005 Microsoft released antivirus and antiphishing filters that are an integral part of their new operating system. ISPs also have begun adding more security features directly to their servers to provide an added layer of protection for their subscribers. Apple computers are well regarded for their lack of vulnerability to viruses and other malware. The low instances of attack on Apple computers is largely because Apple owners represent only about 10 percent of the computer-owning population; for this reason, it is more efficient and productive for cybercriminals to focus on writing programs to attack PCs.

Software developers also are exploring the possibilities of introducing randomization of code into some programs; by creating coding that is less predictable, it will be more difficult for hackers to figure out how to break into a computer or server. According to computer expert Chris Fleizach:

other interesting proposals have included traceback systems that can remove the anonymous identity of data traveling through the Internet, devising a system for fast and accurate discovery of the source of even one packet of data. Stopping distributed denial of service attacks and worm discovery has also been proposed as a method that can be automated and integrated into the backbone of the Internet, high speed routers. By analyzing similar patterns coming from separate locations, such detectors can realize an attack while it is in its infancy and isolate infected hosts.[37]

As computer forensics and cybercrime both advance in the future, there is no doubt that the chase through cyberspace will continue. As long as the technological means remain available to those who wish to break the law, these tools are bound to be put to criminal use. Computer crime investigators can only hope to keep cybercrime in check so that it does not become an epidemic.

Notes

Chapter 1: What Is Cybercrime?

1. David S. Wall, *Cybercrime: The Transformation of Crime in the Information Age*, Cambridge, England: Polity, p. 50.

2. M. E. Kabay, "The Equity Funding Fraud," *Network World Security Newsletter*, January 21, 2002, *www.networkworld .com/newsletters/sec/2002/01190226.html*.

3. *Brian Prince*, "Sarah Palin's Private E-Mail Reportedly Hacked by Activists," eWeek .com, September 17, 2008, www.eweek .com/c/a/Security/Sarah-Palins-Private-Email-Reportedly-Hacked-by-Activists.

4. Quoted in Sophie Borland, "MI5 Warns Firms over China's Internet 'Spying,'" *Telegraph* (London), April 12, 2008, www.telegraph.co.uk/news/world-news/1571172/MI5-warns-firms-over-China's-internet-'spying'.html.

5. Wall, *Cybercrime*, p. 17.

6. Chris Hale, "Internet Crime Is Increasing," in *Does the Internet Increase the Risk of Crime?* ed. Lisa Yount, Detroit, MI: Greenhaven Press, 2003, p. 13.

Chapter 2: The Chase Through Cyberspace

7. Carl J. Franklin, *The Investigator's Guide to Computer Crime*, Springfield, IL: Charles C. Thomas, 2006, p. 73.

8. Matt Richtel, "In the Pursuit of Cybercriminals, Real Detectives Rely on Amateurs," *New York Times*, May 17, 2000, http://query.nytimes.com/gst/full-page.html?res=9802E1D81F3BF934A 25756C0A9669C8B63&sec=&spon= &pagewanted=all.

9. George Crump, "Data Retention: Why Internet Companies Need to Develop a Strategy," Internet Evolution, November 28, 2007, www.internetevolution.com/ author.asp?section_id=545&piddl_ msgid=151143.

10. "Fighting Identity Theft in California," *Los Angeles Times*, September 3, 2008, www .latimes.com/news/opinion/editorials/la-ed-data3-2008sep03,0,6143253.story.

11. "Justice: Hackers Steal 40 Million Credit Card Numbers," CNN.com, August 5, 2008, www.cnn.com/2008/ CRIME/08/05/card.fraud.charges/ index.html.

12. Eoghan Casey, *Digital Evidence and Computer Crime: Forensic Science, Computers and the Internet*, 2nd ed., San Diego, CA: Academic Press, 2004, pp. 17–18.

13. Dario Forte, "Strategic Aspects in International Forensics," in *Forensic Computer Crime Investigation*, ed. Thomas A. Johnson, Boca Raton, FL: CRC Press, 2006, p. 180.

14. Casey, *Digital Evidence and Computer Crime*, p. 19.

15. Casey, *Digital Evidence and Computer Crime*, p. 495.

16. Franklin, *Investigator's Guide to Computer Crime*, pp. 181–82.

17. Franklin, *Investigator's Guide to Computer Crime*, pp. 185–86.

Chapter 3: Trapping the Cybercriminal

18. Matthew Tanase, "Sniffers: What They Are and How to Protect Yourself," SecurityFocus, February 26, 2002, www.securityfocus.com/in-focus/1549.

19. John R. Vacca, *Computer Forensics: Computer Crime Scene Investigation*, 2nd ed., Hingham, MA: Charles River Media, 2005, p. 529.

20. Vacca, *Computer Forensics*, p. 616.

21. Honeynet Project, "Know Your Enemy: Honeynets," Honeynet Project, May 31, 2006, www.honeynet.org/papers/honeynet.

22. Mark Jewell, "*Study: Many Retailers' Wireless Data Systems Easy to Hack*," *USA Today*, November 16, 2007, www.usatoday.com/money/industries/retail/2007-11-15-retail-hacking-study_N.htm.

Chapter 4: Gathering the Evidence

23. Marjie T. Britz, *Computer Forensics and Cyber Crime: An Introduction*, Upper Saddle River, NJ: Prentice Hall, 2004, p. 177.

24. U.S. Department of Justice, "Searching and Seizing Computers and Obtaining Electronic Evidence in Criminal Investigations," U.S. Department of Justice, Computer Crime and Intellectual Property Section, Criminal Division, September 15, 2008, www.usdoj.gov/criminal/cybercrime/s&smanual2002.htm#_IC. p. 117.

25. Curt Bryson and Scott Stevens, "Tool Testing and Analytical Methodology," in *Handbook of Computer Crime Investigation: Forensic Tools and Technology*, ed. Eoghan Casey, San Diego, CA: Academic Press, p. 117.

26. Britz, *Computer Forensics and Cybercrime*, p. 170.

27. Benjamin J. Romano, "Microsoft Device Helps Police Pluck Evidence from Cyberscene of Crime," *Seattle Times*, April 29, 2008, http://seattletimes.nwsource.com/html/microsoft/2004379751_msftlaw29.html.

Chapter 5: Making the Case

28. Vacca, *Computer Forensics*, p. 228.

29. Britz, *Computer Forensics and Cybercrime*, p. 203.

30. *Britz, Computer Forensics and Cybercrime*, p. 205.

31. *Franklin, Investigator's Guide to Computer Crime*, p. 197.

32. Brian D. Carrier, "A Brief Introduction to the Computer History Model," File

System Forensic Analysis, January 21, 2008, www.digital-evidence.org/hist_model1.html.

33. Carrier, "A Brief Introduction to the Computer History Model."

34. Fred Cohen, "Challenges to Digital Forensic Evidence," in *Forensic Computer Crime Investigation*, p. 175.

35. Cohen, "Challenges to Digital Forensic Evidence," p. 177.

36. Cohen, "Challenges to Digital Forensic Evidence," p. 177.

37. Chris Fleizach, "Future Trends in Cybercrime," in "Cybercriminal Activity," written by Hemavathy Alaganandam, Pravin Mittal, Avichal Singh, and *Chris Fleizac*, UCSD class paper, December 6, 2005, http://sys-net.ucsd.edu/~cfleizac/WhiteTeam-CyberCrime.pdf.

Glossary

black hat: A computer savvy criminal who uses his or her knowledge to crack into computers and network systems for illegal or mischievous purposes.

botnet: A network of zombie computers that have been compromised by malware. Botnets are controlled remotely by cybercriminals who use them to help spread viruses, worms, and spam to other computers.

cookie: A text file identifying a computer user who has visited a Web site. This information is stored so that when a visitor returns to a Web site he or she has visited before, the process of using shopping carts, forms, or other features is streamlined.

cracker: A computer hacker who launches computer attacks for illegal reasons. Crackers are not necessarily as computer savvy as black hats.

data diddling: Deliberately altering data on a computer.

DDoS (distributed denial of service): A computer attack against a network or Web site that works by overwhelming a computer system with random information that causes the access gateway to shut down. This prevents outside users from accessing the network or Web site.

guru: An expert white hat.

hacker: Someone who knows how to access a network or Web site remotely, usually for the purpose of proving his or her technical skill.

hacktivist: A hacker or cracker who accesses a Web site and alters it in some way as a form of political protest.

honeynet: A more sophisticated honeypot.

honeypot: Any computer system, Web space, or network of computer data designed to entice a hacker or cracker and reveal his or her methods of breaking in.

imaging: Using software to create a duplicate of the contents of a computer.

malware: Software, such as trojans and worms, designed to cause damage or extract information from a computer.

phishing: Using e-mails or other Internet communication to lure targeted computer users to provide financial or other personal information about themselves.

samurai: A white hat who is for hire to those who need an expert to find out if computer systems are vulnerable to hackers and crackers.

script kiddies: Inexperienced hackers and crackers who use prewritten scripts to perform computer crimes.

sniffer program: A program designed to monitor Web site and network traffic and collect data about people who are accessing it.

social engineering: Using nontechnical means, such as e-mails that pretend to be from trusted sources and ask for personal information, to lure people into a scam.

spoofing: Pretending to be a trusted source of e-mail, such as a person or institution, in order to gain a computer user's trust and prompt him or her to download malware or visit a fake Web site.

trojan: A type of virus program that does not damage a computer, but rather prepares a gateway that makes the computer vulnerable to a virus later.

virus: A malicious program designed to damage a computer or extract information from it.

white hat: An ethical computer hacker who is motivated to access computers by a desire to prove his or her technical skills, or sometimes to help private individuals or companies discover vulnerabilities in their networks.

wizard: A renowned and highly regarded white hat.

worm: A type of virus that can reproduce itself.

zombie: A computer that has been infected by a virus and can now be controlled by a malicious outside user.

For More Information

Books

Joe Anastasi, *The New Forensics: Investigating Corporate Fraud and the Theft of Intellectual Property*. Hoboken, NJ: Wiley, 2003. This book has twenty chapters, each one portraying a legal case about fraud and theft that involved the use of computer forensics to solve.

Marjie T. Britz, *Computer Forensics and Cyber Crime: An Introduction*. Upper Saddle River, NJ: Prentice Hall, 2004. A thorough look at the history, laws, and forensic procedures involving computer crime and computer forensics, this book is intended for readers interested in pursuing a career in computer forensics.

Peggy Daniels, ed., *Policing the Internet*. Detroit, MI: Greenhaven Press, 2007. This book provides pro and con discussions about the ethical and legal problems posed by controlling the content of and access to the Internet.

Karen Judson, *Computer Crime: Phreaks, Spies, and Salami Slicers*, rev. ed. Berkeley Heights, NJ: Enslow, 2000. This is an overview and history of computer crime that describes the rise of the technology used and the people who committed the crimes.

Peter Lilley, *Hacked, Attacked and Abused: Digital Crime Exposed*. London: Kogan Page, 2002. This book is intended for readers interested in protecting themselves from cyberattacks.

Lisa Yount, ed., *Does the Internet Increase the Risk of Crime?* Detroit, MI: Greenhaven Press, 2006. This book offers opposing viewpoints about how and whether the Internet has led to more crime in society.

Web Sites

Carnegie Cyber Academy (www.carngie cyberacademy.com/index.html). This Web site is designed for young adults, offering information on how to "be good cybercitizens and Cyber Defenders of the Internet."

HowStuffWorks (www.howstuffworks.com). This Web site offers explanations of how various things work, written in nontechnical language. It includes a section on "How Computer Forensics Works."

U.S. Department of Justice (www .cybercrime.gov). This is a U.S. government site that provides news articles about cases involving cybercrime.

Index

Picture Credits

About the Author

Kevin Hile is a freelance writer, editor, and Web site designer based in Michigan. A graduate of Adrian College, where he met his wife, Janet, he has been a reference book editor for almost twenty years. Hile is the author of *Animal Rights* (Chelsea House, 2004) and *Little Zoo by the Red Cedar* (Strategic, 2008). He also is the author of *Dams and Levees*, *Ghost Ships*, and *Centaurs* for KidHaven Press and *César Chávez* for Lucent Books.